# Contents

# 'And the Glory of the Lord' from the oratorio *Messiah* (1742) by George Frideric Handel (1685-1759)

- 'Messiah' is an **oratorio** (musical work based on words and stories from the Bible)
- Text taken from the book of Isaiah, Chapter 40, Verse 5 (King James Version of the Bible)
- From the **Baroque era** (1600-1750)

## Melody

- Based on **four ideas** (or motifs), each using a section of the text:

**Idea 1**: outline of a **triad**, then upwards **scale** (**syllabic**, or one note per syllable)

**Idea 2**: descending one-bar **sequence** (mainly **melismatic**, or several notes per syllable)

**Idea 3**: **repetitive** idea based on three statements of the **descending fourth**

**Idea 4**: long (dotted minim) repeated **pedal notes**

## Tonality & Harmony

- **Diatonic, major keys** – minor keys avoided – helping to portray the joyful **affection**
- Starts and ends in **a major** ('home key')
- Modulates smoothly to related keys **e major** (**dominant**) and **b major** (**dominant** of **dominant**)
- Most **cadences** are **perfect** – v to i (help to reinforce key changes)
- Some of the perfect cadences are **inverted** (vb>i or vii°b>i) for a less emphatic effect
- Some **imperfect cadences** – i to v(b)
- **Plagal cadence** (IV to I) –at bar 63 and, most obviously, at the very end

## Instruments & Voices

- four-part mixed **chorus**: **sopranos**, **altos** (male in this recording), **tenors**, **basses**
- **String orchestra** doubling vocal lines: **1st violins**, **2nd violins**, **violas**, **'cellos**, **double basses**
- **Continuo** played by **organ** (in this recording - although it could be **harpsichord**) and **'cello**
- **Period instruments** and **Baroque tuning** used in this recording (A=415Hz)

## Texture

- Most of the piece alternates between **homophonic** (block chords)...
- ...and **polyphonic** (two or more tunes at once)
- Different numbers of parts together – 1, 2, 3 or 4
- **Imitation** used – for example, at the first appearance of Idea 2 ('shall be revealed')
- **Doubling** of parts (eg. Tenors and basses singing Idea 4 'for the mouth of the Lord' for the first time)
- Two different musical ideas together (e.g. Sopranos and altos singing Idea 3 in the same passage)
- Briefly **monophonic** – first three notes of first alto phrase and a soprano entry (doubled by violins) towards the end (both using idea 1 – 'And the glory of the Lord')

## Rhythm & Tempo

- **Allegro** (fast) tempo marking until last three bars, which are marked **Adagio** (slow)
- 3/4 **time signature** (three crotchets per bar)
- Sprightly dance rhythms (often **dotted**)
- **Hemiolas** (grouping of accented beats 2+2+2 instead of 3+3) used in lead-up to cadences

## Dynamics

- **Terraced dynamics** (i.e. Sudden, not gradual, changes)
- Only a few dynamic markings in score, either *p* or *f*
- In this recording, the movement ends loudly

## Structure

- There is no set form; instead, the four ideas are weaved together in a variety of textures:

| Bar | Orch/Voices | Ideas | Texture | Key | Cadence |
|-----|-------------|-------|---------|-----|---------|
| 1 | Orch | 1, 2 | Homophonic (later polyphonic with countermelody) | A | Perfect |
| 11 | A | 1 | Monophonic (1st 3 notes), homophonic | A | Perfect |
| 14 | SATB | 1 | Homophonic (four parts) | A | Perfect |
| 17 | T, B, S | 2 | Polyphonic (two parts, imitative) | A>E | Perfect |
| 22 | T, B, S, A | 1, 2 | Polyphonic (two parts) | E | Perfect |
| 33 | SATB | 1, 2 | Homophonic (four parts) | E | Perfect |
| 38 | Orch | 2 | Homophonic with countermelody | E | Perfect |
| 43 | A, T | 3 | Homophonic (one line at a time, imitative) | A | Perfect |
| 51 | T+B, S+A | 4, 3 | Homophonic (T/B unison pedal, S/A sixths) | A | Perfect |
| 58 | S, A+T+B | 4, 3 | Homophonic (S inverted pedal, ATB) | A | Plagal |
| 64 | A, T, B, S | 3, 4 | Homophonic (imitative, four parts, two ideas together) | A>E>B | Perfect |
| 74 | Orch/SATB | 1 | Homophonic (orchestral interlude, then with voices) | B | Perfect |
| 79 | SATB | 3 (4) | Polyphonic (A/T together, imitated by S/B together) | B | Imperfect |
| 83 | S, A, T, B | 4,3,1,2 | Polyphonic (up to four different ideas together) | B>E | Perfect |
| 102 | A, T, B, S | 3,1,2,3 | Polyphonic (imitative), homophonic, polyphonic | A | Imperfect |
| 124 | S, A, T, B | 4 | Homophonic (with S then S/A inverted pedal) | A | Plagal |
| 134 | SATB | 4 | Homophonic (four parts) | A | Plagal |

# First movement from Symphony No. 40 in G minor (1788) by Wolfgang Amadeus Mozart (1756-1791)

- a **symphony** is a large-scale work for orchestra in several (usually four) movements
- From the **Classical era** (1750-1830)

## Melody

- Well-proportioned, balanced and graceful melody lines; regular four-bar phrases; contrasting melodies in 1st and 2nd subjects
- **1st subject** in home key of **G minor** is based on a repeated and developed **three-note motif**:

- **Bridge section** modulates to related key (**relative major**), ending in imperfect cadence in Bb major

- **2nd subject** characterised by 'pathetique' (melancholy) mood because of chromatically descending motif; in Bb major, then **codetta** ending with perfect cadence in Bb major

-

## Tonality & Harmony

- Largely diatonic harmony - uses I, II, IV, V(7), VI – but some chromatic chords as well
- **EXPOSITION** (repeated in this recording)
- **DEVELOPMENT** explores the 1st subject (or fragments of it) in 12 different keys:
  - After a **chromatic modulation** via a **diminished 7th** chord, the development begins in the distant key of F# minor
  - The bass line then descends **chromatically**, **modulating** into E minor
  - From E minor, the keys change every two bars in a **circle of fifths**: A minor, D minor, G minor, C major, F major, Bb major (loud **contrapuntal tutti** with **countermelody** of **staccato** quavers alternating between violins and lower strings/bassoons)
  - There are then a series of **dominant pedals** of D minor, Bb minor, C minor, and finally the home key of G minor (quiet homophonic dialogue between strings and woodwind)
- **RECAPITULATION** is almost all in the home key of G minor:
  - **1st subject** in home key of G minor, with an imperfect and perfect cadence leading into…
  - **bridge section** is longer than in the exposition; it briefly explores Eb major and F minor, but ends in home key of G minor
  - **2nd subject** in G minor, then **coda** ending with perfect cadence in G minor

# Instruments

- **Classical orchestra** consisting of:
    - **Strings**: 1st violins, 2nd violins, violas, 'cellos, double basses – used almost all of the time
    - **Woodwind**: flute, 2 oboes, 2 clarinets, 2 bassoons – more sustained notes
    - **Brass**: 2 horns – written for natural horns (without valves) that only play 7 notes each
    - no trumpets or timpani (the other instruments often appearing in a classical orchestra)
    - **Transposing instruments**: clarinets in Bb, 1st horn in G, 2nd horn in Bb

# Texture

- Mainly **homophonic**
- **Contrapuntal (polyphonic)** section between the melody and the countermelody in the development section, also including **imitation**
- **Dialogue** between strings and woodwind, particularly in second subject and codetta/coda
- Oboes and bassoons provide harmonic filling; parts doubled; use of octaves; orchestral textures varied throughout the movement

# Rhythm & Tempo

- **Time signature** of 4/4 throughout
- **Tempo** marking 'Molto Allegro' – very fast
- 1st subject **motif** of two quavers and a crotchet pervades much of the movement
- Some **dotted rhythms** and **syncopation** to add interest, particularly in the codetta and coda

# Dynamics

- 1st subject mostly quiet (p), apart from a loud outburst
- Bridge section, once established, is mostly loud (f)
- 2nd subject starts quietly (p) but gets louder (crescendo) towards the end
- Codetta/coda alternate
- Development has a loud section in the central contrapuntal section, but starts and ends quietly
- Most dynamics contrasts occur suddenly – only a few crescendos and no diminuendos

# Structure

### Sonata form

| EXPOSITION | | | | DEVELOPMENT | RECAPITULATION | | | |
|---|---|---|---|---|---|---|---|---|
| 1st subject (home key) | Bridge | 2nd subject (related key) | Codetta | 1st and/or 2nd subject explored in a variety of keys, textures and dynamics | 1st subject (home key) | Bridge | 2nd subject (home key) | Coda |
| G min. | → Bb | Bb | Bb | 10 different keys | G min | | G min | G min |

# Prelude No. 15 in D flat major ('Raindrop') from *24 Préludes*, Op. 28 (1838) by Frédéric Chopin (1810-49)

- Chopin's 24 Preludes, Op. 28 are each written in a different major or minor key
- A **prelude** is a brief 'opening' piece which usually precedes another movement (e.g. fugue); however, in this case, each prelude is a stand-alone piece depicting a different mood
- From the **Romantic era** (1830-1900)

## Melody

- **Cantabile** (singable)/lyrical/legato/elegant melodic lines
- Regular **4-bar** or **8-bar phrases**
- Repeated dominant **pedal note** (Ab/G#)
- Two-bar **cadenza** towards the end starts on Bb, the highest note in the piece

## Tonality & Harmony

- Opening Section A is **Db major**, with its own middle section modulating into **Ab major**, the dominant and **Bb minor**, the relative minor; ends with an imperfect cadence
- Section B is **C# minor** (enharmonic tonic minor); also ends with an imperfect cadence
- Repeat of Section A in home key of **Db major**, this time ending with a perfect cadence
- Harmony is largely **diatonic** (i.e. major or minor) with some **chromatic** chords
- Music **modulates** to both related keys (Ab major/Ab minor/G# minor) and unrelated keys e.g. Bb minor
- Some **tonally ambiguous** chords and suspensions in B section, uses 7ths and 9ths

## Instrument

- Like most of Chopin's music, this is written for **solo piano**
- Sustaining **pedal** marked frequently in score for expressive effect
- Exploits the piano's wide **dynamic range**, from pp to ff
- Unlike some of Chopin's other piano pieces, this is **not a virtuoso** prelude

## Texture

- Almost entirely **homophonic**, apart from brief **monophonic** cadenza towards the end
- Repeated dominant **pedal note** (Ab/G#) pervades the whole piece – this is in the middle of the texture in section A (**inner pedal**) and at the top in the first half of section B (**inverted pedal**)
- Accompaniment of **broken chords** in Section A (left hand)
- **Single-line melody** in right hand (treble clef) above accompaniment and pedal notes in Section A
- Melody of **two-note chords** in left hand below pedal notes in Section B then moves to right hand
- Repeated note becomes **reinforced by octaves** in the right hand in the second half of Section B

## Rhythm & Tempo

- **Time signature** of C (common time, or 4/4) throughout
- Tempo/mood marking of **sostenuto** (sustained) – legato, unhurried
- **Ritenuto** ('slow down') at the end of each A section
- **Slentando** (also meaning 'slow down') just before short monophonic **cadenza**

- **Rubato** performance – flexible tempo for expressive effect
- **Repeated quavers** (on dominant pedal of Ab/G#) – 'raindrop' effect
- **Dotted rhythm** characterises melody in section A
- **Longer notes** (mainly crotchets and minims) characterise chordal bass melody in section B
- **Acciaccatura** ('crushed' grace note) then **septuplets** (seven notes of equal length in the space of one beat) at the end of the first phrase
- Another **septuplet** appears towards the end of the first Section A
- One **dectuplet** (ten notes of equal length in the space of one beat) appears towards the end

## Dynamics

- Vary from **pp-ff** (very soft to very loud)
- No sudden dynamic contrasts; many **crescendos** and **diminuendos**
- Opening A section p (soft) throughout
- B section starts **sotto voce** ('under the voice' – like a whisper)
- B section has two **crescendos** to ff (much louder than A section)
- **Smorzando** ('dying away') before **cadenza**, which is marked f (loud); ends **pp** (very soft)

## Structure

- **Ternary form** (ABA), but with a shorter A section at the end
- First A section is also in ternary form in itself (B section starting in Bb minor)
- B Section longer than both outer sections put together

| | Bars | Description |
|---|---|---|
| **Opening section** | 1-4 | First phrase in Db major – legato, sostenuto (sustained) – ends in a perfect cadence; repeated 'raindrops' (Ab) in left hand. Ornamentation at end of phrase: acciaccutura then septuplet |
| | 5-8 | Almost exact repeat of bars 1-4 (without the ornamentation) |
| | 8-12 | New phrase, stepwise melody which modulates into Ab minor (perfect cadence in bars 11-12) |
| | 13-19 | First four bars a variant on the previous four-bar phrase; end of phrase echoed in bars 18-19 |
| | 20-23 | Repeat of first phrase (back in Db major), with different septuplet at end |
| | 24-27 | Almost exact repeat of bars 20-23 (without the ornamentation) |
| **Middle section** | 28-31 | Ominous chorale-like chords in the LH with 'raindrops' in the RH. The key is now C# minor (the enharmonic tonic minor) |
| | 32-35 | Four-bar phrase answering the previous four bars – very similar |
| | 36-39 | Repetition of 28-31, except that the RH is playing 'raindrops' in octaves |
| | 40-43 | Fortissimo, dramatic chord of E major (the relative major of C# minor) |
| | 44-59 | Almost exact repeat of bars 28-43 |
| | 60-63 | C# minor, melody at top of texture; development of the chorale-like melody |
| | 64-67 | G# 'raindrops' continue in octaves in RH; inner harmonies change between I, IV and V (C#m, F#m, G#) |
| | 68-70 | A repeat of bars 60-62 |
| | 71-75 | Briefly modulates in F# minor, then back into C# minor, with repeated chords IV and V over the dominant pedal of G#. Chord IV is major, preparing for... |
| **Recap.** | 76-79 | Db major (original key) – similar to bars 1-4, but with a ten-note ornament (instead of seven) |
| | 80-83 | Starts like bars 5-6, but is interrupted by an unaccompanied melody starting on a *forte* high B flat |
| **Coda** | 84-89 | Coda based on dominant (V) and tonic (I) chords of Db major |

# 'Peripetie' from *Five Orchestral Pieces* (1909) by Arnold Schoenberg (1874-1951)

- **Expressionist** style – expresses intense feelings, ranging from stark terror to lyrical beauty
- Schoenberg founded the **Second Viennese School**, a group of composers which also included **Berg** and **Webern**
- One of the most important features of expressionist music is its **atonality** – lack of key
- Meaning of 'Peripetie' = 'sudden reversal' *changes?*

## Melody

- **Disjunct** (mainly leaps, rather than steps) and angular
- Made up of many short, **fragmented motifs** (there are 7 motifs in the first 18 bars)
- Motifs transformed by techniques such as **inversion** and **augmentation**
- Uses a **hexachord** (a group of six notes)...
- ...and its **complement** (the six notes not used in the first hexachord)
- **Klangfarbenmelodie** literally 'tone colour melody', this describes how timbre contributes to melody in addition to pitch and rhythm

## Tonality & Harmony

- **Atonal** (not in a major or minor key)
- Harmony also uses **hexachords** and their **complements** (see above)

## Instruments

 *– triple woodwind*

- **Woodwind** piccolo, 3 flutes, 3 oboes, cor anglais, clarinet in D, 3 clarinets in Bb, bass clarinet, 3 bassoons, contrabassoon / 1/2/3=1/2/3 players play same notes
- **Brass** 6 horns (open and 'stopped'), 3 trumpets, 3 trombones, tuba / bell up=point the end of brass instrument upwards, to produce a loud, strident sound / sometimes muted
- **Percussion** xylophone (one chord at the beginning), cymbals (played towards the end with a cello bow and then a mallet), tam tam and bass drum (both have one note near the end)
- **Strings** violin I, violin II, viola, 'cello, double bass / pizz.(icato)=plucked arco=bowed divisi=section divided into 2 or more parts

## Texture

- The principal melody is labelled H⌐ (**Hauptstimme**)
- The next most important part is labelled N⌐ (**Nebenstimme**)
- Mostly **polyphonic/contrapuntal** (more than one tune at one)
- Occasional **monophonic** and **homophonic** moments
- Complex textures created from techniques such as **imitation**, **inversion** and **canon** (e.g. end of the piece uses three different canons)

## Rhythm

- The **metre** (time signature) changes between 3/4, 2/4 and 4/4
- The opening contains mainly short **triplet** and **sextuplet** rhythms
- Wide range of note values, from **demisemiquavers** to **semibreves**

## Tempo

- The starting tempo is **Sehr rasch** (very quick)
- Then, later in the first section (A) **etwas ruhiger** (somewhat calmer)
- The second and third sections (B, A1) use the first tempo
- Many solo, more reflective passages are played **rubato** (freer sense of tempo)
- The fourth section alternates (C) between **ruhiger** (calmer) and **heftig** (passionate)
- The fifth section (A2) goes back to the original tempo

## Dynamics

- **Large range** of dynamics, from *ppp* to *fff*
- Many **crescendos** and **diminuendos**, often one of each within a phrase
- **Sudden changes of** dynamics, e.g. the ending goes from *fff* to *ppp* in one bar

## Structure

- **Free Rondo Form** – A B A1 C A2
- The score is very detailed and complicated. Below is a brief overview of what happens in each section.

|  | Instruments (most prominent) | Texture | Tempo markings | Dynamics |
|---|---|---|---|---|
| **A** Bar 1 | Whole orchestra introduced in sections over first three bars<br><br>Then 1st Clarinet | Short homophonic bursts<br><br>Thins out for clarinet melody | **Sehr rasch** (very quick),<br><br>**etwas ruhiger** (somewhat calmer) | Starts loud<br><br>Then suddenly quiet |
| **B** Bar 18 | Cellos<br>1st Trumpet<br>then many others | Polyphonic, complex<br><br>Thickens towards end | **Tempo** (=Sehr rasch) | Starts quietly<br>Immediate crescendo<br>Melody always loud |
| **A1** Bar 35 | Strings – rising leaps<br><br>6 Horns - hexachord | Strings in octaves<br><br>Horns homophonic | **Tempo** (=Sehr rasch) | Quiet, crescendo<br><br>Loud, then quiet |
| **C** Bar 44 | 1st bassoon<br>Solo cello<br>Woodwind<br>Most of the orchestra | Sparse texture for first part<br><br>Suddenly much thicker | **Ruhiger** (Calmer)<br>**Heftig** (passionate)<br>**Ruhiger**<br>**Heftig**<br>**Ruhiger** | Quiet<br>Loud<br>Quiet<br>Very Loud<br>Quiet |
| **A2** Bar 59 | Clarinets + strings<br>Then all others in quick succession | Quickly thickens for final tutti | **Tempo** (=Sehr rasch) | Starts very quiet<br>Crescendo to v. loud<br>Ending very quiet |

# 3rd Movement (Fast) from *Electric Counterpoint* (1987) by Steve Reich (1936-)

- **Minimalist** style (American, 1960s to present)
- Uses these minimalist techniques:
  - **motif/cell** – short, repeated, distinctive fragment of a melody
  - **ostinato** – repeated pattern
  - **note addition** – building up a melody by repeating it and adding a few notes at a time
  - **rhythmic displacement** – shifting a rhythm so it starts in a different place in the bar
  - **layering** – building up a texture one layer at a time
  - **canon** - exact imitation of a motif or melody, overlapping with its first occurence
  - **resultant melody** - where one instrument plays the highest-pitch note in the rest of the contrapuntal texture (e.g. live guitar part from bar 20)

## Melody
- **Three motifs** (or cells) used:
  - Live Guitar/Guitars 1-4 play a **melodic motif** based on **hexatonic** (six-note) scale: E F# G A D B E
  - Bass Guitars play a **bass motif** based on three notes: A C E
  - Guitars 5-7 play (strum) interlocking **chordal motif** (C, Bm, E5, D)
- **Guitars 1-4** and **Live Guitar** play **motif** Live guitar later plays **resultant melody** of the four-part canon
- Bass guitars build up, using note addition, to **bass motif** based on three notes: A C E
- In the final section, **Guitars 1-4** and **Live Guitar** play melodic **motif** (like at the beginning)

## Tonality & Harmony
- The piece is **tonal/diatonic**, but it does not use harmony in a traditional/functional way (i.e. it avoids conventional chord progressions and cadences) and has a **static harmony**
- **Tonal ambiguity** at start – **G major/E minor**
- The bass guitars draw the tonality towards **E minor**
- When the key changes to C minor/Eb major, **Guitars 1-4** and **Live Guitar** change to a slightly different hexatonic scale: Eb F G Ab Bb C D

## Instruments
- **8 electric guitars** (1 live, 7 pre-recorded)
- **2 bass guitars** (both pre-recorded)
- The studio technique of **panning** is used – one bass guitar is heard from the left speaker and the other from the right

## Texture
- Piece is almost entirely **polyphonic** (hence 'counterpoint' in title)
- First bar and a half **monophonic** (guitar 1 only), stating melodic motif
- Then **layering** is used by the live guitar and guitars 2-3 to create a **four-part canon**
- By definition in a canon, **imitation** is used as the four guitars copy each other
- LIve guitar stops when it is doubled by Guitar 4 and soon plays the resultant melody

## Rhythm & Tempo

- **Tempo** is 'Fast' and the metronome mark is ♩=192
- **Time signature** is **3/2** at the beginning and end
- Towards the end, the time signature changes to **12/8** and back to 3/2 several times, in all parts except Guitars 1-4, which **stay in 3/2**
- Two time signatures at the same time like this are known as a **polymetre**
- 12/8 and 3/2 both contain 12 quavers per bar, so the bars are the same length but with different emphasis and grouping of beats
- The melodic and bass motifs both entirely consist of **quavers** and **quaver rests**
- The melodic and bass motifs are both **syncopated**
- The chordal motif is based on two dotted minims and a dotted semibreve (or equivalent in tied notes), cutting across the bar lines to create a **cross-rhythm**

## Dynamics

- Crescendos and diminuendos used to introduce or remove layers from the texture gradually
- Guitars 1-4 all marked *mf* throughout
- Live guitar is played *f* at first, then fades out – then does the same again
- Live guitar plays resultant melody *p* at first, then crescendos to *f*, then fades out
- Both bass guitars play *f*, then *ff*, then fade out before coda
- Live guitar introduces chordal motif *f*, then twice fades out and comes back in *f*
- Live guitar plays resultant melody *f* until the end, when the final high e is *ff*
- Guitars 5-7 enter *mf* then diminuendo to *p* before the first key change, then fade out before coda

## Structure

This is not a standard structure. There are three main sections (A, B and Coda) and nine shorter sections, defined by changes in texture or key:

| | | |
|---|---|---|
| A | 1 | Guitars 1-4 and Live Guitar enter in turn, playing melodic motif in canon. They build up to four parts with live guitar playing resultant melody |
| | 2 | As before, but the two bass guitars in turn are added to the texture, building up to a three-note bass motif by note addition |
| | 3 | As before, but with the Live Guitar, then Guitars 5-7 in turn, strumming chordal motif |
| | 4 | Now all the instruments are playing, the Live Guitar switches back to resultant melody |
| B | 5 | Sudden key change to C minor/Eb major |
| | 6 | Sudden key change back to E minor/G major<br>Time signature changes to 12/8 (except for Guitars 1-4) then back to 3/2 |
| | 7 | Sudden key change to C minor/Eb major again<br>Time signature changes to 12/8 and back to 3/2 every four bars |
| | 8 | Sudden key change back to E minor/G major<br>Changes in both key and time signature become more frequent<br>Bass guitars and Guitars 5-7 fade out at end of this section |
| Coda | 9 | The final section is similar to the first, with Guitars 1-4 playing the melodic motif in canon and the Live Guitar playing resultant melody |

# 'Something's Coming' from *West Side Story* (1957) by Leonard Bernstein (1918-1990)

- *West Side Story* is a piece of **musical theatre** composed by Leonard Bernstein in 1957
- It is based on Shakespeare's tragic play ***Romeo and Juliet***
- Two rival street gangs: **Jets** (Americans) and **Sharks** (Puerto Rican)
- **Tony** (the Romeo character) used to lead the Jets with Riff, but now wants to 'go straight'
- **Maria** (the Juliet character) is the sister of the gangleader of the Sharks, Bernardo
- Music for the **Jets** is influenced by **jazz** and **blues** (popular among young Americans in the 1950s)
- Music for the **Sharks** influenced by **Latin** music (e.g. mambo, cha-cha)
- 'Something's Coming' uses quiet dynamics, 'push' rhythms, and timbre to create a feeling of **anticipation** (Tony is actually about to meet Maria at the dance at the gym)

## Melody
- Short two-bar phrases and narrow range of a 6th in opening section
- Recurring interval (throughout *West Side Story*) of **augmented fourth** (or tritone): e.g. 'Who knows'
- **Jazz** influence in **blue notes** and **seventh chords**

## Tonality & Harmony
- **D major**, with two sections in **C major**

## Voice & instruments

> These are the instruments played in the accompaniment of 'Something's Coming'. Other woodwind and percussion instruments are played elsewhere in the score.

- **Solo tenor voice** (character of Tony)
- **Woodwind**
  - 3 **Clarinets** and **Bass clarinet** in Bb
  - 3 of the above players change to **flutes** for the section starting at 'whistling down the river'
  - **Bassoon**
- **Brass**
  - 2 **Horns** in F
  - 3 **Trumpets** in Bb – playing with cup mutes
  - 2 **Trombones** – playing with cup mutes
- **Rhythm section**
  - **Drum kit** (bass drum, snare drum with sticks and later brushes, and hi-hat)
  - **Piano**
  - **Electric guitar**
  - 2 **Double Basses** (pizzicato throughout)
  - **Celesta** – glockenspiel played with keyboard (only in the section 'the air is humming')
- **Strings**
  - 7 **Violins** - split into three groups playing **pizzicato**, later **bowing** and playing **tremolo**
  - 4 **Cellos** in unison – starting **pizzicato**, later **bowing** in unison
  - **Harmonics** accompany 'Come on, deliver' and 'the air is humming'

## Texture

- **Melody-dominant homophonic** (tune plus accompaniment)
- **Layered** textures of independent parts
- Clarinets play repeated **syncopated riff** (accents reinforced by pizz. violins) in 3/4 sections
- Rhythm section plays **'oom-cha' accompaniment** in 2/4 sections

*tremolo – can feel like 6/8*

## Rhythm

- **Time signature** alternates between **3/4** and **2/4** (3 and 2 crotchets per bar)
- **Syncopation** – off-beat rhythms
- **Push quavers** – type of syncopation in jazz which anticipates the beat by a quaver
- **Riff** – distinctive, syncopated repeated melodic and rhythmic motif
- **Cross-rhythms** – e.g. 'around the corner' melody in long triplets against 'oom-cha' accompaniment

## Tempo

- **Fast - 176 bpm** (beats per minute) throughout

## Dynamics

- The dynamics range from **ppp** to **f**
- Each smaller section of music has its own dynamic level
- Most sections contrasting strongly with the previous section (see table below)

## Structure

- This is not in a standard verse-chorus form
- There are several music ideas in the overall form **Intro – A – B – B1 – A1 - Outro**

| | | Key | Instrumentation/Texture | Time sig. | Dyn. |
|---|---|---|---|---|---|
| | Introduction | D | Clarinets playing syncopated riff | 3/4 | pp |
| A | 'Could be. Who knows?' | | Pizzicato violins reinforcing accents of riff Bass clarinet, cellos, double basses and drum kit keeping 3 beats in a bar | | |
| | 'It may come cannonballing' | | Muted brass and rhythm section | 2/4 | f |
| | 'Who knows? It's only just' | | *Same music as 'Could be. Who knows?'* | | pp |
| | 'I got a feeling' | | *Same music as 'It may come cannonballing'* | | f |
| B | 'Could it be? Yes it could' | C | Clarinets playing countermelody Rhythm section playing 'oom-pah' | 2/4 | p |
| | 'Something's coming, I don't know what it is' | | Above plus muted brass | | f |
| | 'With a click, with a shock' | | *Same music as 'Could it be? Yes it could'* | | p |
| | 'Something's coming, don't know when, but it's soon' | | *Similar to previous 'Something's coming' except it is a tone higher, over the pivot chord of G to move back into D* | | f |
| | 'Around the corner' | D | Flutes/strings playing high countermelody Rhythm section continues 'oom-pah' | 2/4 | mf |
| B1 | 'Will it be? Yes it will' | C | *Same as 'Could it be? Yes it could'* | | ppp |
| | 'Come on something' | | *Same as 'Something's coming, don't know when'* | | f |
| | 'The air is humming' | D | Violins 1-4 (tremolo)/celesta countermelody Violins 5-7 playing harmonics Rhythm section continues 'oom-pah' | 2/4 | p |
| A1 | 'Who knows? It's only just' | | *Shorter version of 'Could be. Who knows?'* | 3/4 | dim. |
| | Outro | | *As above, with Tony sustaining 7th note (C)* | | fade |

# 'All Blues' from the album *Kind of Blue* (1959) by Miles Davis (1926-1991)

- • **Modal jazz** style (more laid-back reaction to the frenetic bebop style of the 1940s)

## Melody
- • **Modal** – the head and most of the solos are based on the **G mixolydian mode** = GABCDEFG
- • Some **blue notes** used, e.g. F on G major chord, F#/E# and G/F# in extended chords
- • **Head** (composed melody) characterised by a rising major sixth but otherwise mostly conjunct
- • **Solos** (improvised melodies) are played by one instrument at a time. The muted trumpet plays the head (two choruses) and improvises a solo (without mute) for four choruses, then the alto and tenor saxophones each improvise a solo lasting for four choruses, then the piano improvises a solo lasting for two choruses before the head (two choruses) and coda played by the muted trumpet.

## Tonality & Harmony
- • For the Head and Solos, *All Blues* uses a version of the **12-bar blues** chord sequence in G:

| G7 | G7 | | G7 | G7 |
|----|----|----|----|----|
| C7 | C7 | | G7 | G7 |
| D7#9 | Eb7#9 | D7#9 | G7 | G7 |

- • **Seventh chords:**    **G7** = G B D F    **C7** = C E G Bb
- • **Extended chords:**    **D7#9** = D F# A C E#        **Eb7#9** = Eb G Bb D# F#   **chromatic** and **dissonant**

## Instruments
- • **Frontline** (main solo instruments):
  - ○ Miles Davis: **trumpet** (played with a **Harmon mute** in the head, but not in the solo)
  - ○ Julian 'Cannonball' Adderley: **alto saxophone** (wide **vibrato** in solo)
  - ○ John Coltrane: **tenor saxophone** (almost **no vibrato** in solo)
- • **Rhythm section** (main accompanying instruments):
  - ○ Bill Evans: **piano** ('**comping**' or improvising accompanying patterns during solos)
  - ○ Paul Chambers: **double bass** (plucked)
  - ○ Jimmy Cobb: **drum kit** (played with **brushes** to begin with, later with **sticks**)

## Texture
- • **Melody-dominant homophonic**, with several **layers** built up one at a time in the introduction and first head:
  - ○ **Rhythm section: drum kit** (played with brushes), **bass** (playing a **riff** based on **G7 broken chord**) and **piano** (playing trill with both hands, which stops after the introduction)
  - ○ **Riff in thirds** around middle C played by the two saxophones. This riff continues under the head and, as a four-bar section, punctuates the head and solos later on. It is played by the piano instead of the saxophones after each of the frontline solos. The riff is replaced by piano **comping** during the solos.
  - ○ **Melody** (see above)

## Rhythm & Tempo

- **Time signature 6/4** throughout (compound duple metre)
- **Tempo** marking **Jazz waltz** (similar feel to 2 bars of 3/4)
- Tempo (not marked in score) is **156 crotchets (or 52 dotted minims) per minute**
- **Swing quavers** – first quaver of each beat is roughly twice as long as the second
- **Syncopation** (off-beat rhythms) used a lot, especially in solos
- **Rhythmic displacement** to make the most of short melodic motifs (especially in tenor saxophone solo)
- The head contains mostly **long notes** – these **become shorter** as the solos progress

## Dynamics

- Head is **p** with **crescendo/diminuendo** in bars 5-6 and 9-10 of the twelve-bar blues sequence
- Solos contain contrasts of **p** and **f**, with **crescendos/diminuendos** and occasional **accents** and **sforzandos**
- The song **fades out** at the end

## Structure

Based on **12-bar blues** chord sequence repeated **19 times**, interspersed with **4-bar link** (shaded below):

| Intro | 4 bars | **Rhythm section**: drum kit establishes jazz waltz feel, bass begins riff, piano plays trill in both hands |
|---|---|---|
| Link | 4 bars | Both **saxophones play riff** in thirds. Rhythm section continues as before. |
| Head | 12 bars | The texture above continues while the **muted trumpet** plays the melody |
| Link | 4 bars | Riff in thirds played by saxophones above rhythm section |
| Head | 12 bars | As for the previous head, with variations to the melody and rhythm |
| Link | 4 bars | Riff in thirds played by saxophones above rhythm section |
| Solo | 4x12 bars | **Trumpet** (unmuted)<br>Short, syncopated motifs |
| Link | 4 bars | Riff in thirds played by piano with rest of rhythm section |
| Solo | 4x12 bars | **Alto saxophone**<br>Short notes, angular, disjunct, chromatic, wide range, virtuosic, wide vibrato |
| Link | 4 bars | Riff in thirds played by piano with rest of rhythm section |
| Solo | 4x12 bars | **Tenor saxophone**<br>Fast scales, quick runs, rhythmic displacement, virtuosic, almost no vibrato |
| Link | 4 bars | Riff in thirds played by piano with rest of rhythm section |
| Solo | 2x12 bars | **Piano**<br>Calmer, simple melody in 1st chorus; parallel chords in 2nd chorus |
| Link | 4 bars | Riff in thirds played by saxophones above rhythm section |
| Head | 12 bars | The **muted trumpet** plays the head as before, with slight developments of the melody |
| Link | 4 bars | Riff in thirds played by saxophones above rhythm section |
| Head | 12 bars | As for the previous head, with further minor developments of the melody |
| Link | 4 bars | Riff in thirds played by saxophones above rhythm section |
| Outro | 12 bars | A final improvised solo, this time on the improvised trumpet over the saxophone riff and piano trill. The piece fades out at the end. |

# 'Grace' from the album *Grace* (1994) by Jeff Buckley (1966-1997)

- **Rock** style from the USA
- Influenced by **folk**, **jazz** and *qawwali* (Pakistani religious chant)
- Jeff Buckley's only album; he drowned in a swimming accident three years later

## Melody
- **Wide vocal range** - starts in low register, very high in places, especially during final improvisation
- Melody is mainly **diatonic** with some **chromatic** notes

## Tonality & Harmony
- **Ambiguous tonality** at first: starts on Fm chord but then settles into **E minor**
- **Chromatic** chord sequence in verse and chorus using two chords at the same time:
  - **Em** on the upper three open strings: G, B, E
  - **F5-Em5-Eb5 power chords** (i.e. no middle note) on the lower three strings
- **Rising bass line** underpins chords in pre-chorus: Em-B7/F#-Em/G-A-Bm-A (repeated)

## Voice, Instruments and Technology
- **Lead vocals**: male voice (Jeff Buckley). Vocal techniques include:
  - **Word-painting** (using voice to depict meaning of words) – e.g.
    - Verse 1: **'cries'** set to the melodic interval of a falling 5th
    - Middle 8/Bridge: **'pain'** and **'love'** sung in a fraught way in high register
    - Verse 3: **'slow'** sung to a long note
    - Outro/coda: **'drown my name'** accompanied by a very thick texture
  - Mostly **syllabic** (one note per syllable) with some **melismatic** (several notes per syllable) words (e.g. 'love' in verse 1 and 'fire' in chorus)
  - Some **portamento** (sliding from pitch to pitch) e.g. on 'away', 'afraid' and 'die'
  - **Falsetto** (male voice singing high and sounding like a woman's or child's voice)
  - **Vocalise/vocables/vocalisation** (wordless singing) in bridge section on *oh*, *eeh*
  - **EQ** applied to voice when lyrics return, producing a 'telephone voice' effect
  - Vocal **improvisation** towards the end of song – growling, shouting, distressed, distorted voice
  - **Unaccompanied** vocal at the very end (showing influence of *qawwali* music)
- **Backing vocals (overdubbed** – recorded later to thicken texture/add harmony)
- **2 electric guitars** and one **acoustic guitar** - guitar effects and techniques used:
  - **drop D tuning** - bottom E string tuned down to D
  - **strumming** (notes of chords played together) / **picking** (pattern of notes played separately)
  - **vibrato** – effect adding slight fluctuation of pitch
  - **slide** – moving left hand between frets while the string is still vibrating
  - **distortion** - effect making sound rougher and harsher
  - **whisper** - pick the note with the volume turned down, then turn the volume up quickly
  - **reverb** – the effect of the sound reflecting off surfaces in a performing space
  - **delay** – repeating the sound more quietly very soon afterwards

- flanger – effect producing a sweeping sound, ranging from 'swirling' to 'jet plane'
- **palm muting** - Plucking strings while dampening them with the hand
- **hammer-on** - Sounding a note with the left hand by striking it on the fingerboard
- **pull-offs** - Pulling the string off the fingerboard with the left hand
- **pick scrape** - Moving the edge of the pick along a wound string
- **distortion** - deliberately fuzzy sound as if the volume is turned up too high (twice)
- **bass guitar**
- **drum kit** – bass drum, snare drum, tom toms (used for **rolls**), hi-hat cymbal, crash cymbal
- **synthesizer** (using **modulation** – slight variations of pitch – at the beginning)
- **strings** using these techniques:
  - **pizzicato** (plucked)
  - **col legno** (played with the wooden part of the bow)
  - **tremolo** (separate rapid repetitions of a very short note created by 'shaking' the bow)

## Texture
- The main texture is **melody-dominant homophonic** (melody and accompaniment)
- Textures are **varied** throughout:
  - Electric guitars and drums feature virtually throughout
  - Bass/drums and acoustic guitar are taken out in the introduction and links
  - String parts only used from time to time

## Rhythm, Tempo & Dynamics
- Time signature **12/8** (quadruple compound metre) throughout
- Tempo: dotted crotchet = **64 bpm**
- **Cross rhythms** e.g. between the bass guitar and his voice on the words 'clicking of time'
- Vocal line enters on an **anacrusis** (upbeat)
- Frequent **syncopation** in vocal and bass lines
- **No dynamic markings** in score, but the song becomes louder towards the end

## Structure
- **Verse-chorus** structure with a pre-chorus linking verses 1 and 2 with their choruses
- **6-bar intro/link** before each verse (shaded below)

| Intro | First three bars Fm Gm Em (guitar picking) |
| | Next four bars repeat D A7 (guitar strumming) |
| Verse 1 | 'There's the moon asking to stay' Em Em/F5 Em/Eb |
| Pre-chorus 1 | 'My fading voice sings of love' Em F#dim G6 A6 Bm A6/9 Em (repeated) |
| Chorus | 'Wait in the fire' (sung four times) uses Em/F5 Em Em/Eb (repeated) |
| Link | Same as intro, but with a mandolin effect on the acoustic guitar |
| Verse 2 | 'And she weeps on my arm' Em Em/F5 Em/Eb |
| Pre-chorus 2 | 'And the rain is falling' Em F#dim G6 A6 Bm A6/9 Em (repeated) |
| Chorus | 'Wait in the fire' (sung four times) Em/F5 Em Em/Eb (repeated) |
| Middle 8 | Vocalise 'ooh'/'eh' harmonised by backing vocals, paralletl chords: Eb F G F# F Em |
| (or Bridge) | 'It reminds me of the pain' with 'telephone' EQ effect applied (pre-chorus chords) |
| Link | Same as intro, but with the rhythmic, percussive sound of hitting the deadened acoustic |
| | guitar strings and then the acoustic guitar body |
| Verse 3 | 'And I feel them drown my name' – much higher vocal range uses Em Em/F5 Em/Eb |
| Outro | Vocal and guitar improvisation based on chorus; unaccompanied voice at end |
| (or Coda) | |

# 'Why Does My Heart Feel So Bad?' from the album *Play* (1999) by Moby (1965-)

- **Electronic dance** or **club dance** style
- Influenced by **gospel** music (as both vocal samples are taken from a 1953 gospel record)

## Melody
- **Male vocal sample** in verse ('Why does my heart feel so bad?')
- Melody in the verse uses the **A dorian** mode: A B C D E F# G A
- **Female vocal sample** in chorus ('These open doors')
- Melody in the chorus uses the **C major** scale: C D E F G A B C

## Tonality & Harmony
- The verse is **modal** (Dorian mode) and the chorus is in **C major**

- Chord sequence in verse (**A section**):  Am  Em  G  D
  (Amazing Emily Goes Dancing)
- 1<sup>st</sup> chord sequence in chorus (**Bx section**):  C  Am  C  Am

- 2<sup>nd</sup> chord sequence in chorus (**By section**):  F  C  F  C
- The chord sequence is varied later in the verse by the addition of **sus2** and **sus4** chords

## Instruments & Technology
All of the sounds in this song are electronically produced:

- Proformance **sound module** for piano sound
- Yamaha **synthesisers** for synth pad, synth riff and strings sounds
- Roland **synthesiser** for bass sound
- Roland **drum machine** for percussion sounds
- Akai **sampler** for male and female vocal samples (taken from a 1953 gospel choir record):
  - **Male sample** 'Why does my heart feel so bad' is used for the verse (A sections) – this sample is not 'cleaned up', as it contains **electronic ghostings** from the original recording
  - **Female sample** 'These open doors' is used for the chorus (B sections)
- Yamaha **multi effects processor** produces the following digital effects:
  - **Delay** repeats the sound quietly after a short time, usually a fraction of a second (like an echo)
  - **Reverb** gives the impression of the sound reflecting off surfaces to give a sense of a performing space
  - **EQ** (equalisation) reduces or boosts certain frequencies (pitches)
  - **High-pass filter** removes lower frequencies (pitches)
  - **Panning** directs the sound to left or right stereo loudspeakers

## Texture
- Song is completely **homophonic**

- The **layers** enter from the beginning of the song in the following order: piano, male sample, drum machine and synth riff, bass and synth pad
- One-bar **breakdown** (all sounds stop apart from continuing effects) after second verse
- Second verse begins with a thinner texture of female vocal sample and static synth chords
- Similarly the outro uses a thinner texture of male vocal sample and static synth chords

## Rhythm, Tempo & Dynamics

- **Time signature 4/4** throughout
- **Tempo** marking of **98 bpm** (beats per minute)
- Piano part is more **syncopated** from section A5
- **No dynamic markings** in score – contrasts are provided by changes in texture

## Structure

Moby himself describes this song as having a **verse-and-chorus** structure, which the Edexcel Textbook and Anthology label as A and B sections respectively. Each smaller section below (apart from the one-bar break at bar 73) is **eight bars long** and is based on a four-chord sequences (each chord is played for two bars before changing). Each layer is based on an 8-bar **loop** (ostinato).

| Main section | Smaller section | Brief description |
|---|---|---|
| INTRO | A1 | **Piano** plays chord sequence **Am Em G D** (two bars each) |
| VERSE | A2 | As above, adding **male vocal sample** 'Why Does My Heart Feel So Bad' |
| | A3 | As above, adding **drum machine** and **synth riff** |
| | A4 | As above, adding **bass** and **string-synth chords** |
| | A5 | As above, but with piano playing **syncopated** variation of original pattern using **sus2** and **sus4 chords** |
| CHORUS | Bx1 | All the above instrumental sounds, but **female vocal sample** 'These open doors' replaces male sample over **C Am C Am** chord sequence (two bars each) |
| | By1 | As above, but with a different chord sequence: **F C F C** (two bars each) |
| VERSE | A6 | As for A5, but this time with the male vocal sample echoed in a 'telephone voice' using **delay** and **EQ** effects |
| | A7 | Exact repeat of A6 |
| BREAK | | A one-bar **breakdown** during which **delay**, **EQ** and **reverb** effects can all be heard |
| CHORUS | Bx2 | **Female vocal sample** (sounding more distant with lots of **reverb** and **delay**) accompanied by **static synth chords C Am C Am** (no piano or drums) |
| | By2 | Exact repeat of By1 |
| | By3 | Exact repeat of By1 |
| OUTRO | A8 | **Male vocal sample** accompanied by **static synth chords** only (no piano or drums) |

# 'Skye Waulking Song' from the album *Nadurra* (2000) by Capercaillie

- **Folk fusion** style (i.e. traditional **folk** mixed with more modern **pop** music)
- The lyrics, the folk style and the band are from **Scotland**; the language is **Gaelic**
- **Skye** is an island off the coast of Scotland
- **Waulking** is a traditional treatment of tweed cloth; hence a 'waulking song' was a song sung by women working on the cloth – it would have a **strong rhythm** and **call-and-response**
- **Lyrics** are from a lament based on an Irish legend (sad lyrics/mood, slow tempo, modal)

## Melody

*vocables – check proper name. scotch snap*

- The (vocal) melody is **pentatonic** (GABDE) – could be E minor or G major pentatonic scale
- Phrase A – three bars long, high in voice – starts on high D; response ends on G
- Phrase B – one bar long, low in voice – starts on low D; response ends on high D

## Tonality & Harmony

- The accompaniment uses the chords **G, Em, C** and, in one bar only, **Am7**
- The tonal centre could be G major or E minor, but their dominant chords (D or B) are avoided, so the song sounds **modal**
- The song starts with the synthesiser playing a **cluster chord** based on Em (E, F#, G, A, B)
- The introduction and most of the verses use the chord sequence **Em-G**
- Verses 4 and 8 use the chord sequence **C-G-Em-C-G**
- Verse 7 uses the chord sequence **Am7-Em-Em-G**
- The outro alternates between the chords of **C** and **G**

## Voice & instruments

- **Solo female singer** (singing quite low – the melody is notated as if for a male tenor!)
- **4 Folk instruments:**
    - **Uilleann pipes** (like small bagpipes) –play in the instrumental middle 8 and verses 4 and 8
    - **Accordion** ('squeezebox')
    - **Bouzouki** (a plucked string instrument, traditionally used in Greek folk music)
    - **Fiddle** (folk music name for a violin) – plays **tremolo** in introduction
- **6 Pop/rock instruments:**
    - **Synthesiser** – with **modulation** (in this sense meaning the pitch fluctuates slightly)
    - **Electric guitar**
    - **Acoustic guitar**
    - **Bass guitar**
    - **Drum kit**
    - **Electric piano** (Wurlitzer)

## Texture
- Piece is mainly **melody-dominant homophonic**
- The instrumental middle 8 is **hetereophonic** as the **uilleann pipes** and **fiddle** play two variants of the same melody at the same time
- **Call-and-response** is used within the solo vocal line

## Rhythm & Tempo

- Time signature **12/8** throughout (four beats in a bar, compound métre)
- Frequent **syncopation** in vocal line and instrumental countermelodies
- Hi-hat plays an **off-beat shuffle rhythm** in the introduction
- When the full band enters, the whole drum kit clearly emphasises the 12/8 metre

## Dynamics
- No dynamic markings in the score
- Most verses performed at around *mp*; full band verses are *f*
- Whole song fades out at the end

## Structure
- The song contains 8 verses. The shaded verses (4 and 8) is where the full band plays.

| Bar | Section | Brief description |
|---|---|---|
| 1-8 | Intro | Quiet dynamics<br>Sustained cluster chord for keyboard at beginning<br>Fiddle tremolo on D<br>Bar 3 drum kit, bass and Wurlitzer piano come in<br>Hi hat shuffle rhythm off the beat; metre is ambiguous<br>Chords G and Em established by end |
| 9-11 | Verse 1 | Phrase A (three-bar phrase) |
| 12-15 | Break | Echo of A and instrumental (fiddle tremolo again) |
| 16-20 | Verse 2 | Phrase B  (one-bar phrase) |
| 21-24 | Verse 3 | ABAB<br>Last line unaccompanied |
| 25-28 | Verse 4 | Fuller texture - whole band joins in<br>Backing vocals<br>Chords change to C G Em C G<br>Uses phrases A and B |
| 29-32 | Verse 5 | Same as previous section with accordion adding countermelody |
| 33-36 | Verse 6 | Phrase A with variant (top G) |
| 37-43 | Instrumental | Uillean pipes and fiddle in heterophonic texture |
| 44-48 | Verse 7 | BA Chord sequence changes to Am7 Em Em G<br>Softer<br>All instruments drop out in last line |
| 49-52 | Verse 8 | Full band<br>Chords return to C G Em G |
| 53-65 | Outro | Chords alternate between C and G<br>Improvised  vocals<br>Long fade |

# 'Rag Desh' by Anoushka Shankar (2001)/ Chirangji Lal Tanwar (2004)/ Steve Gorn (2004)

- This set work is from the **Hindustani** tradition of **Northern India** (as opposed to the Carnatic tradition of Southern India)
- **Rag** or **Raga** = a piece of Indian classical music based on a particular pattern of pitches (see below)
- Each raga belongs to a particular time of year and time of day. Rag Desh is associated with the **monsoon (rainy) season** and **night time**
- The **rasa** (mood) is **devotion, romance and longing**
- There are three versions of this set work, performed by the following soloists:-
    1. Anoushka Shankar (sitar)
    2. Chirangji Lal Tanwar (male voice)
    3. Steve Gorn (bansuri) and Benjy Wertheimer (esraj)
- Version 2 is a **bhajan** (Hindu devotional song)

## Melody

- **Rag** or **Raga** = the pattern of pitches used in the piece, like a scale.
- All three versions use **Rag Desh** (as the title suggests), made up of these notes:-
    - Ascending: **C D F G B C** (like a C major scale, except E and A are missed)
    - Descending: **C Bb A G F E D C** (like a C major scale, except B is Bb)
- Melody is **improvised** in the alap but follows a **fixed composition** in the gat/bhajan
- Melody is mainly **conjunct** (stepwise)
- Melody is **decorated** with **tan** (improvised scale-like embellishments)
- **Meend** = slides between notes

## Tonality & Harmony

- No tonality or harmony in the Western sense of the word: just **melody and drone**

## Instruments & voice

- All three versions use **tabla** (pair of hand drums) to keep the beat
- The melody is performed by the following in each version: *sympathetic strings*
    1. **Sitar** (plucked string instrument) — *sympathetic strings*
    2. **Male voice**
    3. **Bansuri** (bamboo flute) and, to begin with, **Esraj** (bowed fretted string instrument)
- In addition to the tabla and melodic instruments, the following instruments accompany:
    1. **Tambura** (bowed string instrument playing drone)
    2. **Sarangi** (bowed string instrument), **Sarod** (plucked string instrument), **Pakhawaj** (long double-headed drum) and [finger] **cymbals** (which play once every 8-beat cycle)
    3. **(Electronic) Tambura** or **Shruti Box** (playing drone)

## Texture

- Layered: **melody** (often improvised), **drum rhythm** (after alap) and often **drone**

# Rhythm

- In all three versions, the opening section, **Alap** (prelude/introduction) is in **free time**
- The rest of each piece (gat or bhajana) uses **Tala** – the metred rhythmic pattern used in the piece, like a time signature:
    1. Gat 1 – 10-beat **Jhaptal** (2+3+2+3) / Gat 2 – 16-beat **Tintal** (4+4+4+4)
    2. Bhajan – 8-beat **Keherwa Tal** (2+2+2+2)
    3. Gat 1 – 7-beat **Rupak Tal** (3+3+2) / Gat 2 – 12-beat **Ektal** (2+2+2+2+2+2)
- **Chand – triplet rhythm** (three equal note-lengths in the space of one beat)
- **Tihai – cross-rhythm** flourish at the end of a section or piece

# Tempo

- In all three versions, the opening section, **Alap** (prelude/introduction) is **slow**
- Each of the following sections is in a fixed tempo as follows:
    1. Gat 1 – **medium**      Gat 2 – **fast**
    2. Bhajan – **medium**
    3. Gat 1 – **slow**      Gat 2 – **fast**

# Dynamics

- All three versions fade in and are very quiet at the beginning
- Alap sections are quiet
- The Gat (versions 1 & 3) or Bhajan (version 2) section is louder
- The Gat (versions 1 & 3) or Bhajan (version 2) section is more varied in dynamics
- There are some **crescendos** and **accents**

# Structure

A raga can have up to four defined sections. In all three versions of the set work, the **Jhor** and **Jhalla** are omitted, but you should be aware of them.

- **Alap** (prelude establishing the notes of the raga, in free time with improvisation)
- **Jhor** (medium tempo with improvisation)
- **Jhalla** (lively tempo with virtuoso improvising skills)
- **Gat** (final section of instrumental raga – a 'fixed composition' with called **tan**)

The three versions all begin with an **Alap**. Versions 1 and 3 (the purely instrumental versions) then both have two **Gats**, whereas Version 2 has a **Bhajan** (Hindu devotional song) instead. Here are the timings:

1. 0.00 **Alap**      0.55 **Gat 1**      9.27 **Gat 2**
2. 0.00 **Alap**      0.50 **Bhajan**
3. Part 1 **Alap**      Part 2 **Gat 1**      Part 3 **Gat 2**      (3 separate tracks)

# 'Yiri' by Koko (2002)

- **Traditional drumming** music from the country of **Burkina Faso** in West Africa
- **'Yiri'** means **'wood'**, possibly referring to the fact that almost all of the instruments are made of wood
- This music is learnt by **oral tradition** and **played from memory** (the score was transcribed afterwards from the recording)

## Melody

- Balaphone and vocal melodies based on a **hexatonic scale** (Gb Ab Bb C Db Eb)
- **Vocal range = 10th** from Gb below middle C to Bb above middle C (tenor range)
- Vocal melody uses mainly **conjunct** (stepwise) movement; balaphone melody uses more leaps

## Tonality & Harmony

- No tonality or harmony in the Western sense of the word, although the melodies are 'in' **Gb major**

## Instruments & voices

*pentatonic notes*

- One high and one low **balaphone** (tuned percussion instrument like a xylophone, with wooden keys and resonating gourds underneath) ['balaphone' is the spelling in the Edexcel textbook; 'balafon' is the French spelling used elsewhere]
- One large and one small **talking drum** (hourglass-shaped drum with the double heads tightened by cords running down the length of the drum; these are tightened under the arm to create changes and slides in pitch, hence the 'talking')
- One **djembe** (goblet-shaped single-headed drum)
- **Male voices:** one **solo singer** and a **chorus**
- A single note on a **bell** at the end of the piece

## Texture

- Piece begins **monophonic** (**high balaphone** solo with **tremolos**)
- Then the two **balaphones** play together in a **heterophonic** texture
- When they first play together and during the coda, the two balaphones play in **octaves**
- For the rest of the piece, the talking drums and djembe play an ostinato and the balaphones play and voices sing in a **layered** texture
- Solo singer often answered by chorus (**call-and-response**, typical in African music)
- Chorus sings in **unison**

- *cross rythms*

# Rhythm & Tempo

- **Time signature 4/4** throughout (apart from the odd 3/4 or 6/4 bar)
- Introduction (high balaphone solo) in **free time**
- After this, a constant '**moderato**' tempo is maintained for the rest of the piece
- The talking drums and djembe play an **ostinato,** the **resultant rhythm** being:
- The djembe occasionally plays **fills** on top of the ostinato
- **Syncopation** is frequently used, especially in the vocal and balaphone parts
- Balaphone rhythms become **more complex** and **syncopated** as the piece progresses
- The balaphone plays **cross rhythms** during one of the instrumental solos
- The vocal soloist makes use of **triplets**

# Dynamics

- No dynamic markings in the score
- Dynamics are largely unvaried (played/sung at about *f*)

# Structure

Most of the piece alternates **vocal sections** with **instrumental breaks**:

| Name of section in Edexcel textbook (if present) | Brief description |
|---|---|
| Introduction | High balaphone monophonic solo, featuring tremolos |
| | Two balaphones – hetereophonic, mainly in octaves |
| | Ostinato begins on the talking drums and djembe |
| Chorus A1 | Voices in unison |
| Break | Instrumental – high balaphone solo |
| Chorus A2 | Voices in unison |
| Break | Instrumental – low balaphone solo |
| | Vocal solo with choral responses |
| | Vocal solo with long held notes |
| | Choral response in unison |
| | Short vocal solo in dialogue with high balaphone |
| | Instrumental break - new melodies on the balaphones |
| Chorus B1 | Full choir singing 'Yiri' with instrumental interjections |
| | Dialogue between voices and instruments |
| | Instrumental break – high balaphone |
| Chorus A3 | Full choir with instrumental interjections |
| | Instrumental break – very syncopated |
| Coda | Five two-bar phrases mostly in octaves, punctuated by rests; bell at end |

# GCSE Music Vocabulary

## Melody

**Scale** – the notes used in a piece in pitch order. Degrees of the major or minor scale:

   I tonic   II supertonic   III mediant   IV subdominant   V dominant   VI submediant   VII leading-note

**Diatonic** – in a major or minor key (as opposed to chromatic, modal or atonal)

**Major** – 'happy' scale made up of tone, tone, semitone, tone, tone, tone, semitone (e.g. CDEFGABC)

**Minor** – 'sad' scale which comes in three versions:

     Natural minor - tone, semitone, tone, tone, semitone, tone, tone (e.g. ABCDEFGA)

     Melodic minor – like natural minor but with sharpened $6^{th}$ and $7^{th}$ notes when ascending

     Harmonic minor – like natural minor but with sharpened $7^{th}$ note

**Chromatic(ism)** – using accidentals not in the key signature

**Tonal(ity)** – describing whether a major/minor key or mode is used

**Pentatonic** – using five notes, e.g. CDEGA (pentatonic major) or ACDEG (pentatonic minor)

**Atonal(ity)** – not using a key at all

**Mode/modal** – similar to a scale, using a different combination of tones and semitones.

     Ionian – CDEFGABC (same as a major scale)

     Dorian – DEFGABCD

     Phrygian – EFGABCDE

     Lydian – FGABCDEF

     Mixolydian – GABCDEFG

     Aeolian – ABCDEFGA (same as a natural minor scale)

     Locrian - BCDEFGAB

**Interval** – the distance between two pitches (semitone, tone, second, third, fourth, fifth, sixth, seventh, octave). Seconds, thirds and sixth can be major or minor; fourths, fifths and octaves can be perfect. Any interval can be augmented (a semitone further away) or diminished (a semitone closer together).

**Conjunct** – a melody using mainly steps (next-door neighbour notes)

**Disjunct** – a melody using mainly leaps (notes that are not next to each other)

**Passing note** – a note in the melody that 'passes' between two chord notes

**Pedal** – a note that is sustained or repeated while the harmony changes (compare **drone**)


## Tonality & Harmony

**Harmony** – combination of different pitches to make different chords

**Chords** – two or more notes sounding together

**Consonant/ce** – notes that sound good together

**Dissonant/ce** – notes that sound bad or clash together

**Triads** – a three-note chord, which comes in four varieties:

     Major triad: 4 semitones + 3 semitones (e.g. C E G)

     Minor triad: 3 semitones + 4 semitones (e.g. C Eb G)

     Diminished triad: 3 semitones + 3 semitones (e.g. C Eb Gb)

     Augmented triad: 4 semitones + 4 semitones (e.g. C E G#)

**Seventh chord** – a triad plus a (usually minor) seventh above the root, e.g. C7 = C E G Bb

**Extended chord** – a seventh chord with an additional $9^{th}$, $11^{th}$ or $13^{th}$ above the root

**Altered chord** – a chord which contains note(s) a semitone higher or lower than those in the scale being used

**Added note chord** – a chord with some extra notes not in the basic chord, e.g. sus2 and sus4

**Cadence** - two chords to end a phrase or section:

      Perfect (V or vii to I), imperfect (I, ii or IV to V), plagal (IV to I), interrupted (V to vi)

**Modulation** – the process of changing key, usually via a pivot chord common to both keys and the dominant of the new key

# Instruments & voices

## Families of the Orchestra etc.

**Strings** – Violin, Viola, 'Cello (short for Violoncello), Double Bass, Harp

**Woodwind** – Flute (piccolo), Oboe (cor anglais), Clarinet (bass clarinet), Bassoon (contrabassoon)

**Brass** – French Horn, Trumpet, Trombone, Tuba

**Percussion** – Timpani, Bass Drum, Snare (or Side) Drum, Triangle, etc.

**Keyboard** – Piano, harpsichord, organ, synthesiser

**Voices** – Soprano (high female), Mezzo-soprano (medium female), (Contr)alto (low female), Countertenor or male alto (falsetto male), Tenor (high male), Baritone (medium male), Bass (low male)

## Pop/rock/jazz instruments

**Electric guitar** – 6 strings tuned, from lowest to highest, EADGBE (see Buckley for techniques)

**Bass guitar** (sometimes called **Electric Bass**) – 4 strings, tuned the same as a double bass (EADG)

**Drum kit** – bass drum, snare drum, ride cymbal (for rhythms), crash cymbals (for effects), tom toms (two mounted and one floor tom), hi-hat (two cymbals clamped together)

**Electric piano** – e.g. Wurlitzer

**Synthesiser** - keyboard playing digital sounds and samples

**Saxophone** – single-reeded woodwind instrument with metal body (both alto and tenor saxophones feature in *All Blues*)

## Folk/world instruments

**Fiddle, Uilleann pipes, Accordion, Bouzouki** – see under Capercaillie

**Balaphone, Djembe, Talking Drum** – see under Koko

**Sitar, Tabla, Bansuri, Esraj, Sarangi, Pakhawaj, Sarod, Cymbals** – see under Rag Desh

## Instrumental and vocal effects

**Vocables/vocalise** – singing

**Melisma(tic)** – several notes to one syllable

**Syllabic** – one note to each syllable of text

**Electric Guitar effects** – see under Jeff Buckley

**Tremolo** – rapidly repeated note (e.g. on a violin) or alternation between two notes (e.g. on a piano)

**Portamento**/slide - moving gradually from one pitch to another

**Vibrato** – effect adding slight fluctuation of pitch

**Slide** – moving left hand between frets while the string is still vibrating

**Distortion** - deliberately fuzzy sound as if the volume is turned up too high

**Pizzicato** – plucking (when applied to bowed strings) – **arco** means return to bowing

## Studio effects

**Sample** – short section of recorded music

**Delay/echo** – digital effect which plays a sound again after a short delay

**Reverb** – complex digital effect which gives the impression of performing in a room or hall

**EQ** (equaliser) – technique of boosting certain frequencies (pitches) in the sound

**Modulation** (in this sense) – slight fluctuation of pitch (e.g. synth at beginning of Capercaillie and Grace)


## Texture

**Monophonic** - unaccompanied melody (could be performed by more than one person)

**Homophonic** - melody and chords

**Polyphonic** - several tunes at once

**Heterophonic** - variations of same tune played at the same time

**Counterpoint**/contrapuntal - several tunes at once

**Imitation** – one instrument/voice copies another (either afterwards or overlapping)

**Canon** – exact imitation of a motif or melody, overlapping with its first occurence

**Layered** – several independent parts performed together

**Call-and-response** – leader plays/sings something, others echo or give an 'answer'

**Unison** – a melody played or sung by two or more performers at the same pitch

**Octaves** – a melody played or sung by two or more performers an octave apart


## Rhythm

**Metre** – the grouping of beats in bars:

> **Duple** – two beats in a bar

> **Triple** – three beats in a bar

> **Quadruple** – four beats in a bar

**Time signature** – the two numbers, one on top of the other, at the beginning of a piece or section of music indicating the metre. The top number indicates the number of beats per bar. The bottom number indicates what type of beat: usually 2 (minims), 4 (crotchets) or 8 (quavers).

**Simple time** – time signature where each beat divides into 2 or 4, e.g. 2/4, 3/4, 4/4, 2/2, 3/2

**Compound time** – time signature where each beat divides into 3, e.g. 6/8, 9/8, 12/8, 6/4

**Free time** – without sense of pulse, e.g. at the beginning of Yiri and Rag Desh


The following note-lengths are based on a crotchet beat (when 4 is the bottom number of the time signature):

> Semiquaver ♬ - ¼ of a beat (half the length of a quaver)

> Quaver ♪ - ½ a beat (half the length of a crotchet)

> Crotchet ♩ - 1 beat (half the length of a minim)

> Dotted crotchet ♩. – 1½ beats (one and a half times the length of a crotchet)

> Minim ♩ - 2 beats (half the length of a semibreve)

> Dotted minim ♩. – 3 beats (one and a half times the length of a minim)

> Semibreve ○ – 4 beats (length of two minims or four crotchets)

**Triplets** – three notes in the space of two

**Syncopation** – off-beat rhythm

**Augmentation** – rhythm or motif repeated with longer note values

**Diminution** – rhythm or motif repeated with shorter note values

**Cross-rhythm** – rhythms that are accented 'across' the metre, for example a hemiola (see below)

**Hemiola** – in triple time, a cross-rhythm of 3x2-beat notes (instead of 2x3-beat notes) in the lead-up to a cadence (particularly used in Baroque music)

## Tempo

**Presto** – very fast

**Vivace** – fast, lively

**Allegro** – fast

**Moderato** – moderate pace

**Andante** – walking pace

**Adagio** - slow

**bpm** – beats per minute, e.g. 60bpm = 1 beat per second

**Accelerando** (accel.) – getting quicker

**Ritardando** (rit.) – getting slower

**Rallentando** (rall.) – getting slower

**Rubato** – literally 'robbed' time, where the tempo fluctuates slightly for expressive purposes

**Pause/Fermata** – held note or rest

## Dynamics

**ppp** (very very quiet), **pp** (very quiet), **p** (quiet), **mp** (moderately quiet)

**fff** (very very loud), **ff** (very loud), **f** (loud), **mf** (moderately loud)

**Crescendo** (cresc.) – getting louder (<)

**Diminuendo** (dim.) – getting quieter (>)

**Decrescendo** (decresc.) – getting quieter

**Sforzando** (sfz) – heavily accented

## Structure

### Popular/folk music

**Intro** (introduction) – first section, usually before main melody begins

**Verse** – repeating section with different words each time

**Chorus** – repeating section, usually with same words each time, more of a climax than a verse

**Middle 8** – section which contrasts with verse and chorus (not necessarily 8 bars long)

**Bridge (pre-chorus)** – section leading into chorus

**Link** – short section joining one section to another

**Outro** – final section

# Classical music

**Binary form** – two contrasting sections (AB)

**Ternary form** – repeated section with contrasting middle section (ABA)

**Rondo form** – initial section recurs after alternating with different sections (ABACA)

**Sonata form** – large-scale ternary form where the outer sections (**exposition** and **recapitulation**) are in binary form (AB) and the middle section (**development**) uses parts of both A and B

**Theme and variations** – Melody which reappears in different versions (A $A_1$ $A_2$ $A_3$ etc.)

**Ostinato** - a short repeating rhythmic/melodic pattern

**Riff** - a short repeating melodic pattern, usually syncopated and particularly in popular music

**Coda** – final section

# About the Listening Exam

- The Listening Exam lasts for **1½ hours**
- **Extra Time** only applies to the last question, so for example 25% extra time gives you 7/8 minutes
- There are **10 questions**, each featuring a **different set work**
- **Questions 1-8** should all be completed and carry 6-10 marks each, split into several short answers
- You have a **choice between questions 9 and 10** – there are 12 marks for each question
- **Questions 1-8 total 68** and question 9/10 is 12 marks, so the total mark is out of 80
- This mark is halved (and rounded up if necessary) to give you a mark out of 40
- This mark out of 40 is added to the two marks out of 30 from your performing and composing to calculate your final percentage for your GCSE Music
- **Grade boundaries**: A*=90%  A=80%  B=70%  C=60%  D=50%  E=40%  F=30%  G=20%

## Questions 1-8

- Questions 1-8 feature two out of the three set works from each Area of Study as follows:-
    - Questions 1-2: Area of Study 1 (Western Classical Music) – Handel, Mozart or Chopin
    - Questions 3-4: Area of Study 2 (Music in the 20<sup>th</sup> century) – Schoenberg, Bernstein or Reich
    - Questions 5-6: Area of Study 3 (Popular music in context) – Davis, Buckley or Moby
    - Questions 7-8: Area of Study 4 (World Music) – Capercaillie, Rag Desh or Koko
- Each of questions 1-8 plays a short excerpt from the set work (about a minute long)
- The excerpt is played several times (anywhere between 2 and 5)
- Questions 1-8 carry 6-10 marks each and add up to 68 out of 80 (or 85% of the total)
- Each question usually takes one of the following forms:
    - Multiple choice (e.g. is the melody major, minor, modal or pentatonic?)
    - Single word answer (e.g. how many beats are there in a bar?)
    - Short response (one sentence)
    - Table to be completed
    - Other types of question, described below

### Expressing opinions

There is usually a question along the lines of: 'Give two **musical reasons** why you like or dislike this piece' (2 marks). For each mark, your answer must contain the following three things:

1. whether you like or dislike the piece (e.g. 'I like the...')
2. a describing word for an element of music that is relevant to the piece (e.g. '...fast...')
3. the element of music itself (e.g. '...tempo')

Examples: 'I like the fast tempo' or 'I dislike the atonal melody'.

### Notation

There is usually a question that asks you to notate part of a melody, rhythm or chord sequence. *The other notes or chords given in the exam are often a clue*, as there is usually some repetition or a pattern of some kind (e.g. a scale) in the missing part.

## Comparison

One of the questions will be based on the comparison of two excerpts from the same set work. You will usually be asked what the similarities and differences are. Make sure any differences you describe mention both excerpts. For example, 'the tempo is faster in the second section than the first section'.

## Listen to the excerpt

What you have learnt and revised about the set work may not apply to the specific extract you hear in the exam. For example, Practice Paper C plays half of the tenor saxophone solo of 'All Blues'. Question 6c asks, 'How many choruses are played in the extract?'. The correct answer is 'two', even though in the tenor saxophone plays four choruses in total in the piece as a whole. Remember, this is a listening exam!

# Questions 9 and 10

- You choose to answer EITHER Question 9 or Question 10 at the end of the exam
- Each of these questions features a set work which does not appear elsewhere on the paper
- Each of the questions is from a different Area of Study (1, 2, 3 or 4)
- There are no listening excerpts for these two questions – you just have to remember!
- Each of these questions falls into three parts: a, b and c
- Questions a and b require short answers (1 mark each) putting the set work into a wider context:
    - In what year was this piece composed?
    - What country does this set work come from? (**USA**, <u>not</u> America, for Reich/Bernstein/Buckley; Burkina Faso for Yiri; Northern India for Rag Desh; Scotland for Capercaillie)
    - What era of music history does this piece belong to? (Baroque, Classical or Romantic)
- Question c is an **extended answer** worth **10 marks**
- You have to comment on the how each of **five given musical features** are used in the set work
- Answer question c by writing **one paragraph** about each of the given musical features
- Question c is the only question that is marked (partly) on **spelling, punctuation and grammar**
- The five given musical features will vary depending on the set work, but they usually include **Melody, Tonality/Harmony, Rhythm, Texture, Structure** and **Instrumentation**
- These are the five features that have been asked about in past and practice papers:
    - **Handel** (Practice Paper A): Melody, Harmony & Tonality, Dynamics, Texture, Mood
    - **Mozart** (2013): Melody, Tonality, Structure, Rhythm, Instrumentation (see next page)
    - **Chopin** (2011): Melody, Dynamics, Texture, Structure, Tonality & Harmony
    - **Schoenberg** (Sample Assessment): Tonality & Harmony, Instruments & Texture, Melody, Dynamics & Tempo, Structure
    - **Bernstein** (2012): Melody, Rhythm, Harmony & Tonality, Structure, Instrumentation
    - **Reich** (Practice Paper C and 2014): Melody, Rhythm/Metre, Texture, Tonality, Instrumentation (2014 only), Structure (Practice Paper C only)
    - **Davis** (Practice Paper A): Melody, Harmony & Tonality, Rhythm, Texture, Structure
    - **Buckley** (2011): Structure, Melody, Harmony, Texture, Instrumentation
    - **Moby** (Sample Assessment, Practice Paper B and 2013): Structure, Harmony/Chords, Melody/Samples, Texture, Technology/Instrumentation
    - **Capercaillie** has not yet come up, but try: Melody, Harmony, Instrumentation, Texture, Structure
    - **Rag Desh** (Practice Paper C and 2014): Dynamics, Instrumentation, Melody, Rhythm, Structure
    - **Koko** (2012): Rhythm, Instruments, Structure, Vocal parts, Texture

# Example extended answer

Comment on how Mozart uses the following elements in the 1st Movement from *Symphony No. 40 in G minor*:

- Melody
- Tonality
- Structure
- Rhythm
- Instrumentation

*Mozart's melodies are typical of the Classical Era. There are well-proportioned, balanced and graceful melody lines, regular four-bar phrases and contrasting melodies in first and second subjects. The first is based on a repeated and developed three-note motif; by contrast, the second subject is based on a chromatically descending motif, creating a 'pathétique' (melancholy) mood.*

*Mozart's tonality is diatonic throughout the movement, although there are occasional chromatic chords. As would be expected in Sonata Form, the movement begins and ends in the home key of G minor. The first subject is in G minor in both the exposition and the recapitulation, whereas the second subject is in Bb major in the exposition and G minor in the recapitulation. The development starts on a diminished seventh chord and modulates through twelve different keys, eventually ending up in G minor for the recapitulation.*

*The movement is in Sonata Form, which has three main sections: exposition, development and recapitulation. The exposition starts without an introduction with the first subject. There is then a bridge section which leads to the second subject. The exposition as a whole ends with a codetta and is usually repeated. The development explores the first subject in a variety of keys, textures and dynamics. The recapitulation has a similar layout to the exposition, except that the bridge section is extended and the second subject is in the home key. The movement as a whole finishes with a coda, which is an extension of the musical material first heard in the codetta.*

*The movement is in common time (four crotchets in a bar) throughout. The motif of two quavers and a crotchet, heard at the very beginning of the symphony, pervades much of the movement. There some dotted rhythms and syncopation to add interest, particularly in the codetta and coda.*

*The instrumentation is for a Classical orchestra with double woodwind (but a single flute) and without trumpets or timpani. The woodwind section is made up of one flute, two oboes, two clarinets and two bassoons; the only brass instruments are the two horns; the strings section is the usual combination of first violins, second violins, violas, cellos and double basses.*

# Past and practice papers

Here is a table of all the past and practice papers in existence so you can test yourself. The numbers in the table refer to the question numbers in the exam. The sample assessment and past papers (including mark schemes, but unfortunately not the recorded excerpts) are available on the Edexcel website. Follow the links from edexcel.com/music > GCSE > Music > Course Materials > Specification > Sample assessments or Exam materials. The latest exam is only available to teachers. The Practice Listening Papers (A, B and C, including CD and mark schemes) are available to order in printed form from the Edexcel and Amazon websites.

| | | Sample Assess. Paper | Practice Paper A | Practice Paper B | Practice Paper C | 2011 | 2012 | 2013 | 2014 | 2015 |
|---|---|---|---|---|---|---|---|---|---|---|
| Area of Study 1 | Handel | - | 9 | 1 | 1 | 1 | - | 1 | 1 | - |
| | Mozart | 2 | 1 | 9 | 2 | 2 | 1 | 9 | 2 | 1 |
| | Chopin | 1 | 2 | 2 | - | 9 | 2 | 2 | | 2 |
| Area of Study 2 | Schoenberg | 10 | 4 | - | 3 | 3 | 3 | - | 3 | 9 |
| | Bernstein | 4 | - | 3 | 4 | 4 | 9 | 3 | 4 | 4 |
| | Reich | 3 | 3 | 4 | 9 | - | 4 | 4 | 9 | 3 |
| Area of Study 3 | Davis | 5 | 10 | 5 | 6 | 5 | - | 5 | 5 | 10 |
| | Buckley | - | 5 | 6 | - | 10 | 6 | 6 | | 6 |
| | Moby | 6, 9 | 6 | 10 | 5 | 6 | 5 | 10 | 6 | 5 |
| Area of Study 4 | Capercaillie | 7 | 7 | - | 7 | 7 | 7 | - | 7 | - |
| | Rag Desh | 8 | 8 (v2) | 7 v1/3 | 10 (v2) | - | 8 (v3) | 8 (v3) | 10* | 8 (v2) |
| | Koko | - | - | 8 | 8 | 8 | 10 | 7 | 8 | 7 |

*in this extended answer, the candidate chooses which version of Rag Desh to write about*

GCSE Music Revision Guide
for the Edexcel Listening exam

© Chris Gill 2015

First edition March 2015
Second edition May 2015
Third edition November 2015

Printed in Great Britain
by Amazon